Most Powe...

this Book belongs to

♡safiyah + ~~███████~~♡

3

ISBN 0 86037 383 5

MUSLIM CHILDREN'S LIBRARY

ISLAM AND SCIENCE FOR KIDS

A Drop of Mercy: The Water Cycle

Authors: *Shahbatun Abu Bakar* and *Nordin Endut*
Graphic Designer: *Azhari Zulkifli*
Coordinator: *Anwar Cara*

Published by

THE ISLAMIC FOUNDATION
Markfield Conference Centre
Ratby Lane, Markfield
Leicester LE67 9SY
United Kingdom
T (01530) 244 944
F (01530) 244 946
E i.foundation@islamic-foundation.org.uk

Quran House, PO Box 30611, Nairobi, Kenya

PMB 3193, Kano, Nigeria

British Library Cataloguing in Publication Data
Abu Bakar, Shahbatun
    A drop of mercy: the water cycle. - (Islam and science for kids)
    1. Hydrologic cycle - Juvenile literature 2. Water - Religious aspects - Islam - Juvenile literature I. Title II. Endut, Nordin III. Islamic Foundation
    551.4'8

Printed by Proost International Book Production, Belgium

A Drop Of Mercy

The Water Cycle

Shahbatun Abu Bakar & Nordin Endut
Designed by: Azhari Zulkifli

The Islamic Foundation

Guidelines for Parents

The objective of these books is to help nurture faith in the hearts of children. By examining the workings of Allah's natural laws from the tiniest cell to the complex universe, it is likely that children will come to understand Allah as the Creator and His Power and His Mercy. In turn, this should awaken the children's awareness of themselves as part of creation, and help to set their feet firmly and joyfully on the straight path *insha' Allah*.

How to use this book

- Provide a good example to the children through an attitude of reverence for Allah, and gratitude for His many blessings.

- Sit with the children in a quiet and comfortable place.

- Read clearly word by word with your finger running under each word.

- Encourage your children to discuss the material, relating it to their experience and understanding.

- When possible, use the Qur'an and Hadith to further develop their understanding. For example *Surah Al-Anbiya'*:30 and *Surah Al-Nur*:43.

- Be patient with the children, results do not happen overnight.

- Help the children find the Qur'anic references on page 29 that describe the water cycle, and let them show how these verses relate to the poster

In the middle of the sea, there is a tiny water droplet floating up and down. It obeys Allah.

High up in the sky, Allah has created the sun to give light and heat to the whole world. Allah is The Most Powerful.

The sunshine heats up the water droplet and turns it into water vapour. The sun obeys Allah. The water droplet obeys Allah too. Only Allah has the power to change the water droplet into water vapour.

The water vapour meets with more water vapour and Allah turns them into cloud. They obey Allah. Only Allah has the power to change water vapour into cloud.

big

heavy

bigger

heavier

biggest

heaviest

More and more water vapour join together. They become bigger and bigger. They become heavier and heavier too. They obey Allah.

The wind is Allah's servant. It obeys Allah. Allah commands the wind to blow the heavy cloud wherever Allah wants it to go. They obey Allah.

Then Allah drops the cloud on dry land as rain. The cloud obeys Allah. The rain comes down as a Mercy from Allah.

Soon Allah makes the dry land come alive. The rain is a blessing to all creatures. Allah has power over everything.

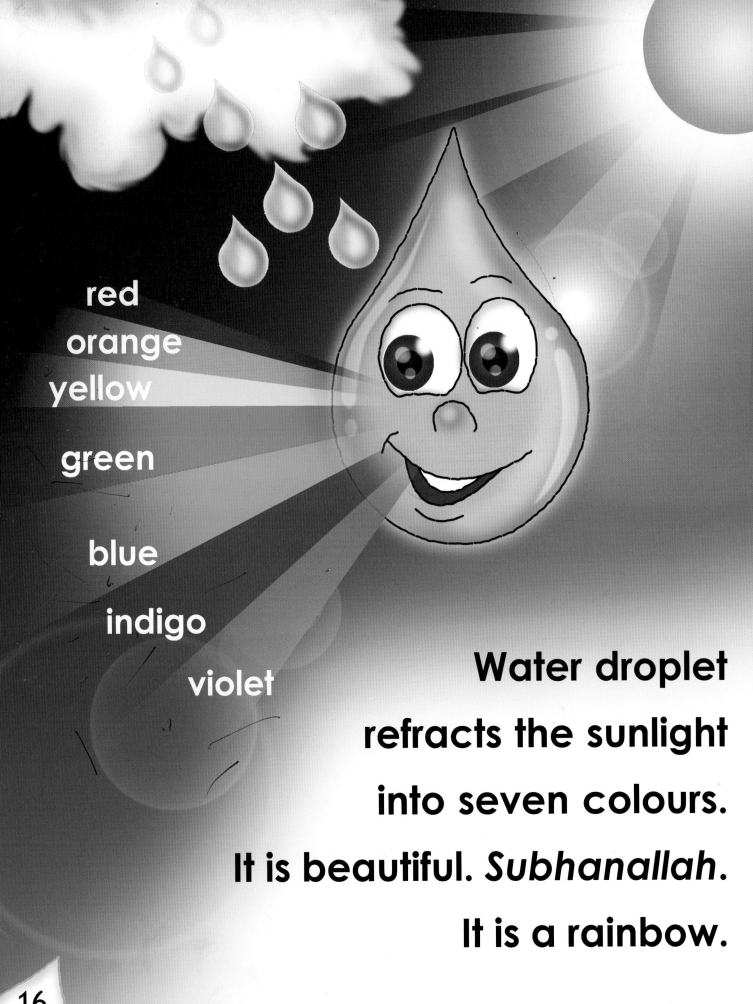

red
orange
yellow

green

blue

indigo

violet

Water droplet
refracts the sunlight
into seven colours.
It is beautiful. *Subhanallah.*
It is a rainbow.

16

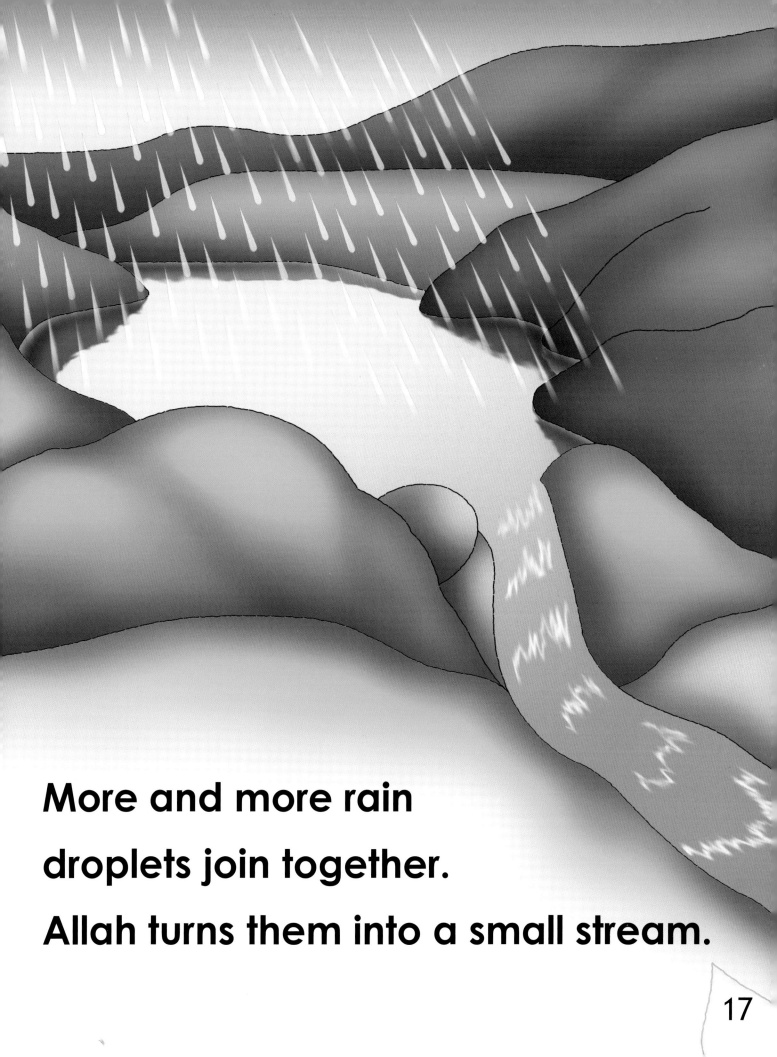

More and more rain
droplets join together.
Allah turns them into a small stream.

17

Allah guides the small stream to join with other small streams. Allah turns them into a small river.

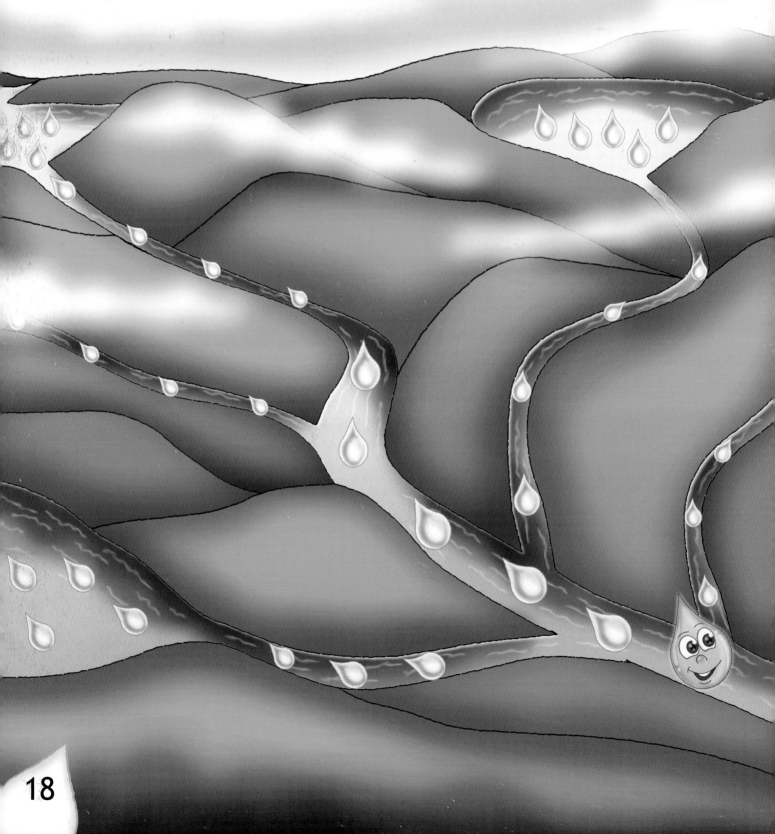

Many small rivers join together. Rivers obey Allah. Then Allah turns them into a big river.

The flowing water can make electricity. The electricity can make our life easier. *Al-Hamdulillah.*

20

Some water droplets evaporate and go up.

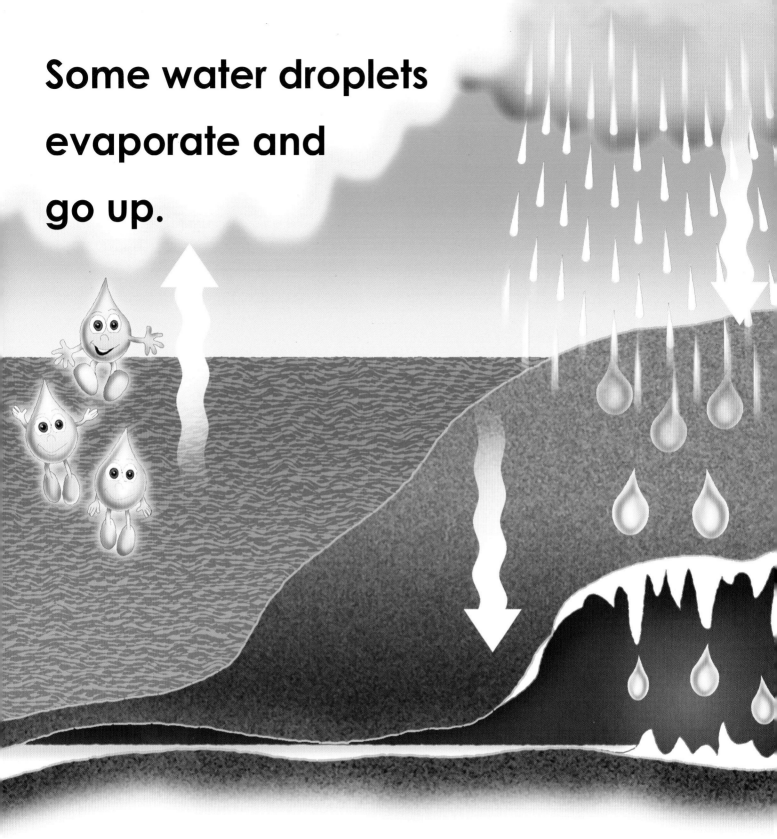

Some water droplets go down and make caves. *Masha' Allah.*

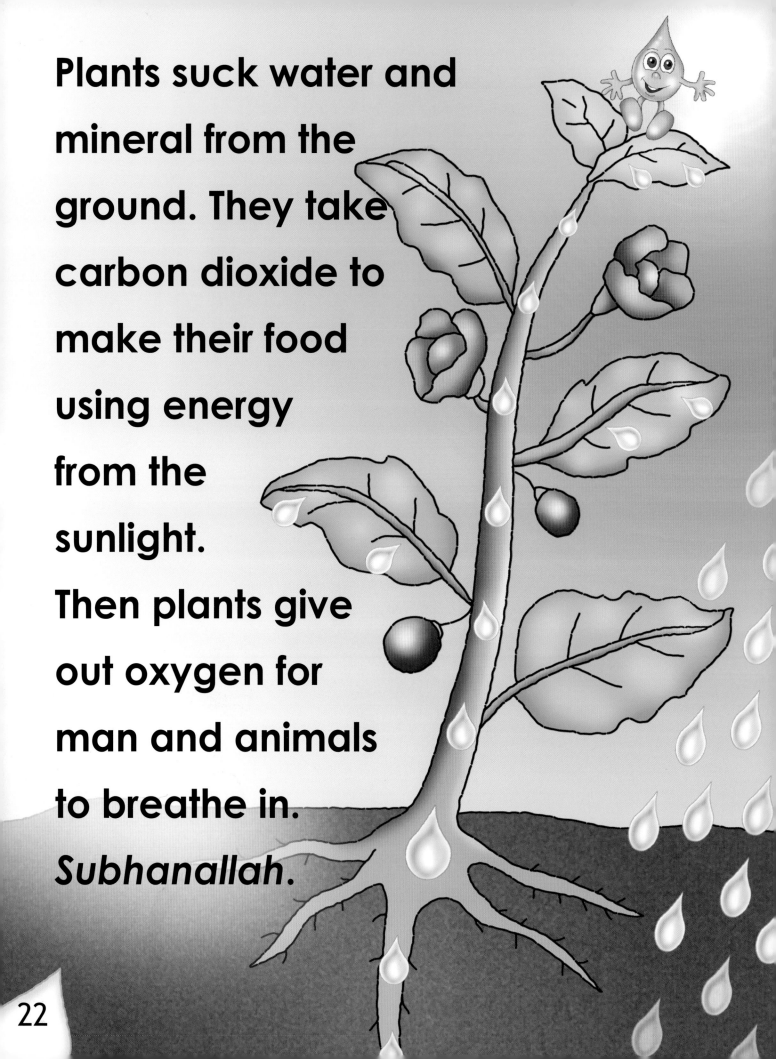

Plants suck water and mineral from the ground. They take carbon dioxide to make their food using energy from the sunlight. Then plants give out oxygen for man and animals to breathe in. *Subhanallah*.

Man needs water to clean his body's system. *Masha' Allah*.

Who needs water?

Everybody needs water.

Wudu

Bathing

24

Washing

Drinking

Cooking

The big river flows back to the sea. At last, the obedient water droplet happily returns home. Everything follows Allah's command.

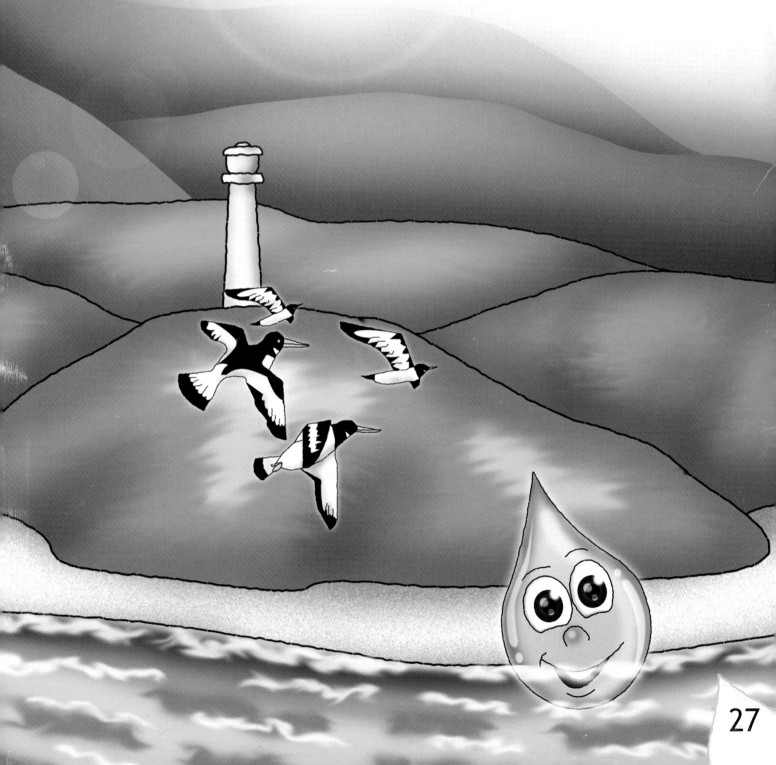

The water droplet says
"I am Allah's servant. I obey Allah."
How about you?

The Water Cycle obeys Allah

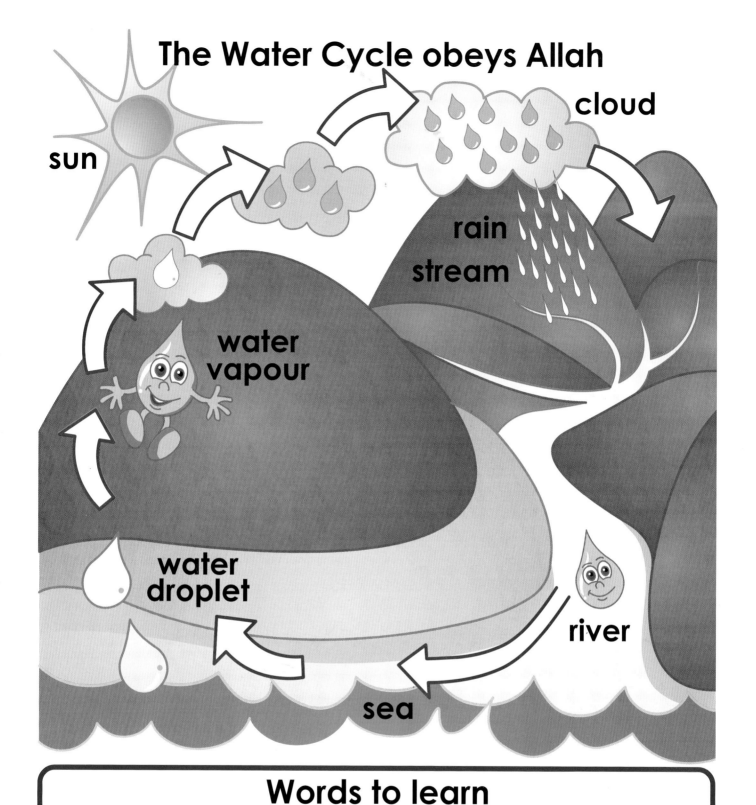

sun

cloud

rain
stream

water
vapour

water
droplet

river

sea

Words to learn

about	blessing	floating	heaviest	refract
alive	blow	flow	light	river
Allah	cloud	follow	mercy	sea
big	command	happy	obey	servant
bigger	creature	heat	powerful	sky
biggest	droplet	heavier	rain	

On the enclosed poster show the places for these Qur'anic references:
[2: 22]; [15: 22]; [13: 17]; [23: 18,19]; [35: 9,27]

Allah is the